EXPERIMENTS with SOUND

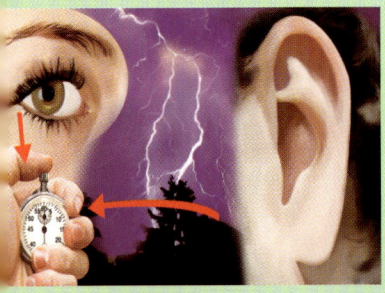

Contents

1. The Sounds Around Us 5
2. Producing a Sound 7
3. Hearing Sounds 10
4. A Sound on Its Way 14
5. Reaching Out 19
6. The Sound of Music 23
7. A Noisy World 29

The Sounds Around Us

Sit quietly, close your eyes, and listen. You will hear all kinds of sounds around you. It could well be a mixture of sounds from the moving fan you are sitting under, the sizzling of food being cooked, the clanging of dishes being washed, the blaring TV of one neighbour competing with the barking dog of another, together with the voices of people and the honking of horns. Even on the laziest and hottest summer afternoon, you can hear the sounds of distant traffic, rustling leaves, chirping birds and the gentle thud of your heartbeat.

Sound can be of two types

Sounds that occur in nature, such as those of animals, trees, people, the wind and the rain, are natural sounds. Those made by radios, televisions, musical instruments, cars and machines are artificial sounds.

Sounds you can make

From singing to snoring and clapping to tapping, one can make all sorts of sounds with the different parts of the body.

How many types of sounds can you make?

Sound can be pleasant or unpleasant

The sounds of gurgling streams, falling rain and twittering birds are all pleasant to the ear. Music has rhythm and is usually pleasant. Pleasant sounds soothe our body and mind.

An unpleasant sound is called noise. A lot of noise is produced in the big cities by men and machines. Too much noise is bad for our health. It can damage our hearing. Noise levels higher than a certain limit cause noise pollution. Even a pleasant sound can turn unpleasant if it is too loud.

Let's go sound tracking

Here is a list of 10 things and the sounds they make, but it is all mixed up. Can you put it in the correct order?

1.	clocks	hoot
2.	fire	rustle
3.	leaves	ring
4.	telephones	squeak
5.	soda-bottles	pop
6.	owls	tick
7.	mice	crackles

Which of these are natural sounds?

Try this

Suddenly increase the volume of a radio or a television set. Observe the reaction of the people in the room.

6

Producing a Sound

You know that sound is produced when you beat a drum or knock at a door. Has it ever struck you that sound is always associated with some kind of movement?

Things that make sound, shake. These shaking movements are called vibrations. The stronger the vibrations, the louder the sound. Have you ever seen vibrations?

Make your own drum

You will need a drum and some grains.

Make the drum by tightly fixing a stretched rubber balloon or a plastic sheet on the mouth of a big bowl.

1. Sprinkle the grains on the drum.
2. Gently tap the skin of the drum. What do you notice?

The vibrations of the drum make the grains dance.

What vibrates when you speak?

Hold your fingers against your throat and say 'aha-aaaaa...'.
Keep raising and lowering the scale, making your voice sound shrill and heavy alternately. Can you feel the sound?

Your throat has a pair of thin sheets of membrane called the *vocal cords*. They vibrate to produce your voice.

How does sound spread?

A sound disturbs the surrounding air by shaking it back and forth very fast. As a result, the tiny particles in the air, called molecules, bump into one another. One air molecule bumps into the next, which in turn bumps into its neighbour, and so on. The individual molecules remain in position and vibrate to and fro. They do not move through the air. But the disturbance, riding on these molecules, spreads out in the form of a wave.

Find out how sound spreads. Try these experiments.

You will need a coiled spring.

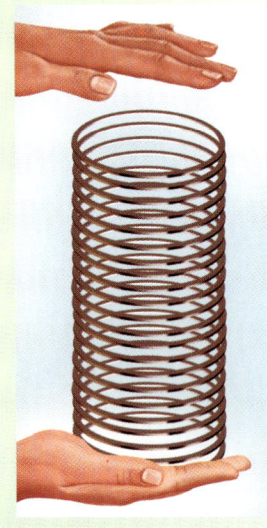

1. Hold the spring by the topmost coil and shake it gently. Watch the vibrations pass down the coils.
2. Shake it every 3 seconds. Observe the vibrations. The coils stretch out and contract alternately. They move only slightly, while the disturbance moves down.

You will need six marbles.

1. Arrange five marbles in a line. They should touch one another.
2. Flick the sixth marble so that it hits the last marble. What happens? Why does the first marble roll away?
3. Now place the five marbles in a line so that they do not touch one another. Flick the sixth marble. Can you explain what you observe?

These marbles are like air molecules. Each marble passes on the disturbance created by the hit to the next marble. The first marble cannot pass it onto any marble, and so rolls away.

Draw a wave pattern

You will need:
- a tuning fork
- hot sealing wax
- fine wire
- a tuning fork stand
- a small pane of glass
- a candle and a matchstick

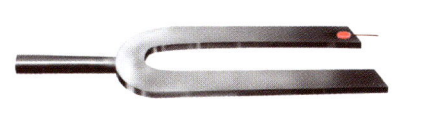

1. Attach a piece of fine wire to a prong of the tuning fork with sealing wax.
2. Clamp the tuning fork horizontally so that it is just above the table top.
3. Hold a small pane of glass above the flame of the candle till it is covered with soot.

4. Place the glass pane on the table with the sooty side up. Adjust its height with books so that the tip of the wire just touches the pane.
5. Draw the books with the glass pane towards you. Pull the books along the edge of the table. This will give you a straight line.

6. Carefully lift the tip of the wire and push the books back to their original position.
7. Now strike the tuning fork horizontally with a pencil. Pull the books towards you once more. Watch the wave traced out by the wire along the straight line.

Hearing Sounds

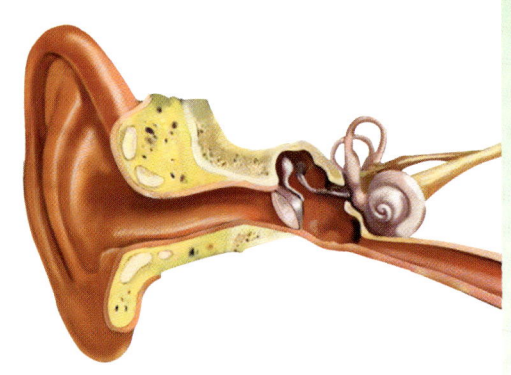

A sound can be heard only when the sound waves reach our ears. Our ear is like a funnel that collects sounds and passes them on to the eardrum. The sound vibrations make the eardrum vibrate. There are some tiny bones that touch the eardrum. These bones vibrate, increase the sound, and carry it further inside.

Compared to us, some animals like dogs, rats, bats, whales and dolphins have a wider hearing range.

Take a look at the ears of animals. How are they different from the human ear? Classify animals, their habits and habitats according to the shape of their ears.

How good is your hearing?

Can you hear the sound of a pin dropping in the other corner of the room? If there are five people in a room wearing watches, can you hear the five watches tick? Can you hear your own heartbeat?

You cannot hear these sounds because they spread in all directions and get lost before they can reach your ears. Air is not a good carrier of sound.

Did you know?

Grasshoppers have ears in their front legs.

Where is the sound coming from?

We can usually tell where a sound is coming from. If a sound is made in front of us, both the ears hear it equally well, and at the same time. If it is made closer to one ear, both the loudness and the time of hearing are different.

Sound sense

1. Choose a volunteer from amongst your friends. Blindfold her/him and stand nearby.
2. Make a gentle noise. The volunteer has to point towards the direction of the sound.
3. Take turns to test your hearing.
4. This can be made more challenging by covering one ear of the volunteer with cotton wool or cloth.

Did you know?

Birds have no outer ear flaps. Their slit-like ears are hidden behind their feathers.

Compared to humans, some animals like dogs, rats, bats, whales and dolphins have a wider hearing range.

Make a tube telephone

You will need:
- two plastic funnels
- a long plastic tube

A soft sound can be heard if it is directed through a narrow channel. Let's see how.

1. Fit the funnels into the two ends of the tube. Make the tube as long as possible. If necessary, tape several tubes together.
2. Give one end of the tube to a friend. Communicate in whispers (from one room to another). The tube will not let your voice spread out and get lost. Do not shout. You may damage your hearing.

Make a stethoscope

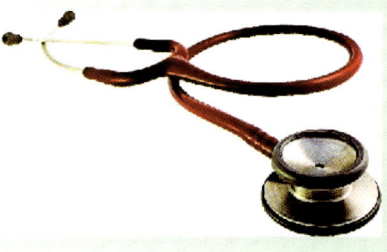

Doctors use stethoscopes to listen to a patient's heart and lungs. Use your tube telephone to hear your friend's heartbeat.

Soft sounds can also be heard by making vibrations pass through something solid. Solids are better carriers of sound than air.

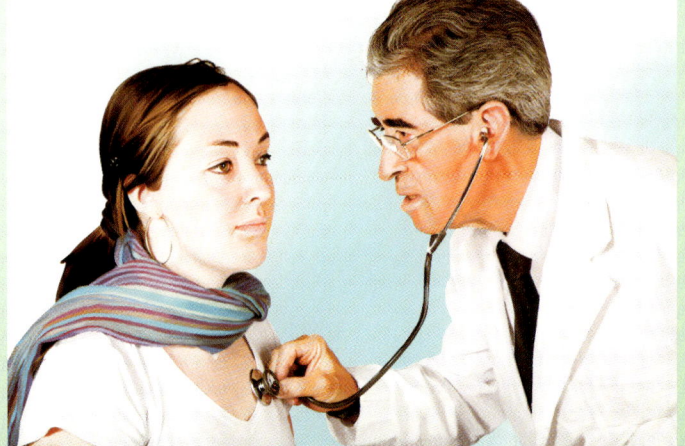

12

Twine telephone

You will need:
- 2 paper cups
- a long piece of twine
- a nail

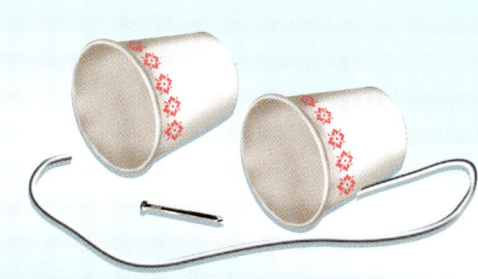

1. With the help of the nail, make a hole in the bottom of each cup.
2. Thread the twine through the holes in the cups and tie a knot at each end to prevent the twine from slipping out.
3. Give one cup to your friend and walk away from each other so that the twine is stretched tight.
4. Speak softly into the cup. Your friend will hear you clearly. Can you tell how this happens?

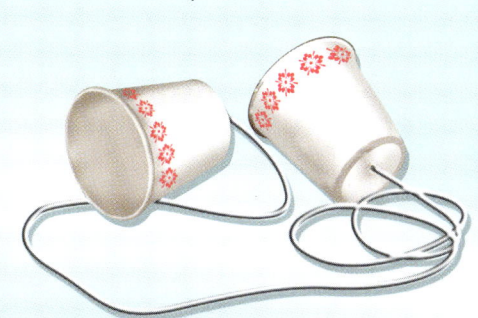

Compare the workings of a Tube Telephone with that of a Twine Telephone.

Rap-tap

You can pass on your secret messages across walls or wooden partitions. Tap your code firmly on one side of the wall. By putting an ear on the other side, your friend can pick up your message.

Water, too, is a good conductor of sound.

Did you know?

Fill a bathtub with water. Lie on your back so that your ears are submerged in water. Keep your mouth and nose above the water. Tap the side of the bath gently. Can you hear the loud booming sound?

A Sound on Its Way

A sound does not reach your ears the instant it is sent out. It takes time to travel from one point to another. You can understand this very clearly during a thunderstorm. Have you noticed that there is a time-gap between a flash of lightning and a clap of thunder? Though lightning and thunder occur together, light travels much faster than sound and so, reaches you earlier.

How far was the lightning?

You can measure the distance of a flash of lightning very easily.
1. Count the number of seconds between a flash of lightning and the first sound of thunder.
2. Divide the answer by three. This gives you the distance, in kilometres, of the lightning.

Let's measure the speed of sound

You will need:
- a friend
- a toy flashgun or a cracker
- a stopwatch and a measuring tape

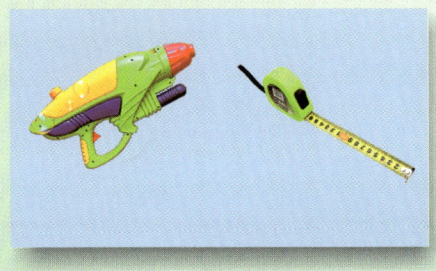

1. On a straight stretch of ground, measure a distance of 500 metres as accurately as possible.
2. Ask your friend to stand at one end with the flashgun or the cracker.
3. You should stand at the other end of the 500 metres with the stopwatch.
4. When you say "Ready", your friend should fire the gun/cracker.
5. As soon as you see the flash of the gun/cracker, start the stopwatch.

6. Stop the watch as soon as you hear the bang. Record the time to the nearest tenth of a second.
7. Repeat steps 4-6 five times, and calculate the average time. (To find the average time, add the five results and divide the sum by 5.)
8. Divide the distance (500 metres) by the average time you have calculated.

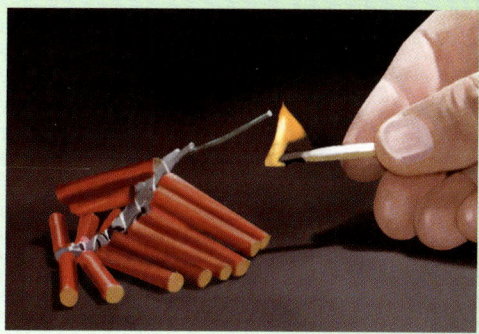

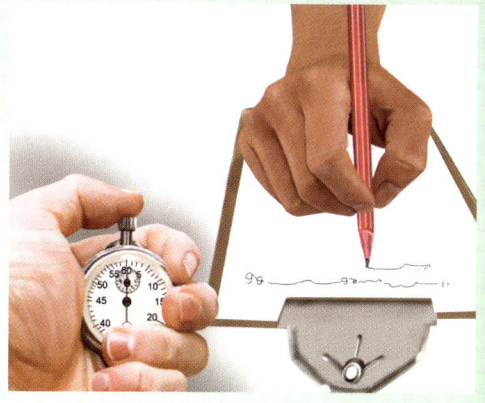

This gives you the speed of sound in air, in metres per second.

Is the speed of sound constant?

A sound wave travels at a speed that depends on the medium through which it is travelling. It travels faster in a denser medium such as water or wood, than in air.

Is it possible to hear in outer space?

In outer space, there is no air with the help of which sound waves can spread out. So it is impossible to hear in outer space.

15

Sound travels faster in a denser medium

1. Place a watch at one end of a table. Sit on the other side of the table. Can you hear the watch ticking?
2. Put your ear to the table. What do you hear? You can hear the ticking very clearly because the wooden table carries the sound waves much better than the air can.

Reflection of sound waves

When a sound wave hits a cliff or a wall, it bounces back and the sound is heard again. This reflected sound is called an *echo*. If the sound gets reflected from different parts of the cliff or the wall, you may hear several echoes. High-domed monuments such as the Whispering Gallery of St Paul's Cathedral, London, also produce good echoes. It is great fun listening to the echo of one's voice.

Try this

You can hear echoes in large empty rooms but not in small ones. Why?

Did you know?

Shoals of fish, submarines and ship wreckages are detected by listening to the echoes of sound waves sent down into the sea. This technique, called SONAR – Sound Navigation And Ranging – can also tell you the depths and contours of seabeds.

There are galleries where even a whisper at one end gets reflected around the wall and is heard on the other side. The Whispering Gallery of St Paul's Cathedral, London, and the Court Room at the Fort of Agra, are two examples of this phenomenon.

Bats prey at night by sending out high frequency sounds and picking up their echoes from objects around them. From the echoes, they can tell the size and position of the various objects.

Cinemas, theatres and concert halls are specially designed, and have huge curtains and padded walls, floors and seats to absorb unwanted echoes so that you can hear clearly.

The Doppler Effect

You must have noticed that sound from the siren of a police car or an ambulance seems to wax and wane as it passes you. This change in the sharpness of sound is noticeable in all moving sources of sound. It is called the *Doppler Effect*.

Why does it happen?

A siren gives out sound waves in all directions. The waves moving in the direction of the vehicle that is towards you, travel at the speed of sound, plus that of the vehicle. So, more waves reach your ears every second than it would if the vehicle was not moving. This gives a sharper than actual sound.

When a train has passed, the sound waves reach you at the normal speed of sound minus the speed of the train. This results in fewer waves reaching you every second, and you hear a drop in the sharpness of the sound.

Verify this next time a train whistles past you.

Reaching Out

Our voice cannot carry itself over long distances. To speak to a large gathering, we need a microphone. A microphone makes our voice louder, or in other words, amplifies it.

Microphone

Next time there is a function in your school or local club, do not miss the opportunity of testing the microphone with whoever is doing a 'mike-test'. Take a closer look at the microphone.
Is it an electrically operated system?
What are the slits meant for?

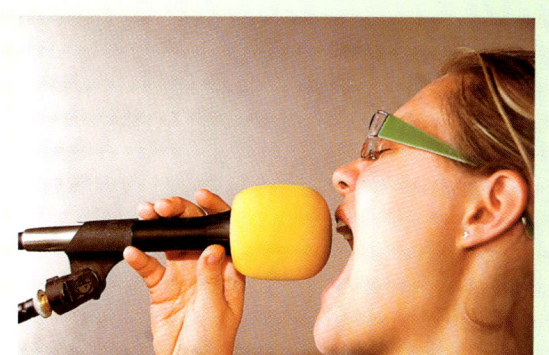

From where does the amplified voice come out? Can you locate the loudspeaker boxes?

How they work

A microphone has a thin metal sheet or diaphragm touching a layer of carbon granules placed on a metal plate. The diaphragm and the metal plate are connected to the two terminals of a battery or power supply.
When you speak into the microphone, the sound waves of your voice vibrate the diaphragm. This makes the

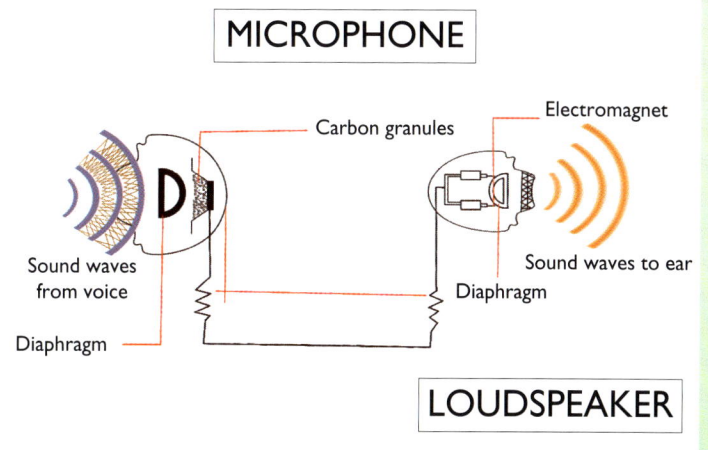

diaphragm press against the carbon granules, more or less, depending on the vibration of your voice. This in turn makes the current flowing through the diaphragm fluctuate. More current flows if the granules are pressed tighter and vice versa. Thus, the current copies your voice pattern.

This is how a microphone changes a sound wave to an electrical signal.

Now it is easy to amplify the electrical signal by passing it through an amplifier circuit. After amplification, a loudspeaker changes the high amplitude electrical signals back to high volume sound waves. A loudspeaker has a metal diaphragm too. The amplified signal is passed through an electromagnet kept beside the diaphragm. The fluctuating current makes the magnet draw and release the diaphragm irregularly. These vibrations give out sound waves.

A telephone helps us to talk to people around the world. The mouthpiece of a telephone handset has a transmitter (much like a microphone), which converts your voice into electrical signals. The earpiece is a receiver which changes the incoming electrical signals to sound waves.

All telephones are connected to the local exchange through a pair of wires to carry the electrical signals back and forth.

Did you know that the electrical supply to a telephone is not from the house supply? That is why a telephone works even during power cuts.

Make your own telephone set

You will need:
- an empty wooden box
- a pocket knife
- pencil and wire
- 2 used razor blades
- a 9-volt battery

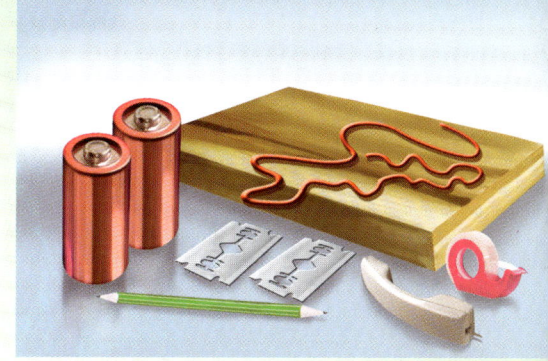

1. Make two slits on the lid of the box with the pocket knife, and fix two used razor blades, as shown in the picture.
2. Sharpen both ends of a pencil. Balance it on the ridges of the blades, making sure that the exposed lead on either side of the pencil is in contact with the blades.
3. Remove an inch of insulation from the ends of two wires. Connect one end of each wire to a blade. Connect the other ends to the battery. If you place your mouth near the pencil and talk, the pencil will vibrate. This will make the current passing through the blades fluctuate.
4. Now, all you need is a receiver and a friend. Get an earphone and connect it to the blades. Take turns to listen.

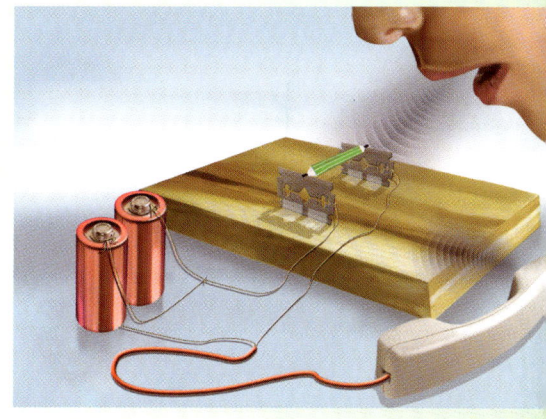

What happens when you make an international call?

When you speak over the phone, transmitting stations superimpose the electrical signal from your telephone onto a kind of wave called a radio wave, and send it out into the sky. Radio waves are specially suited for this job because they travel at the speed of light and, unlike

Radio

sound waves, do not get lost easily. Satellites placed high up in the sky catch these radio waves and send them back to earth. Receiving stations separate out the electrical signal from the carrier, convert it to sound waves, and your friend sitting at the other end of the world hears your voice almost at the same instant!

Radio broadcasts are done through radio waves. Local broadcasts are done through long wavelength (low frequency) radio waves sent along the ground. This is the medium waveband (MW). Long distance transmissions are made through sky radio waves of shorter wavelengths (higher frequencies). These are the short wavebands (SWS).

Here is how you can choose your favourite programme from all the broadcasts around the world.

1. Different stations broadcast their programmes at different frequencies. You must know the frequency in KHz (or wavelength in metres) of your favourite programme and also whether it is a medium or a shortwave programme.
2. Look at the switch panel of your radio receiver set. Switch the radio on, and set the band selector switch.
3. Rotate the tuner. Watch the pointer on the front panel scale. The scale is graduated in metres, KHz and MHZ. Turn the pointer to the frequency of your programme. The circuit inside your radio will do the rest. It will take in only the desired radio wave from the hundreds of radio waves in the air, and convert it to sound for you!
4. Tune the circuit with the fine tuning switch to get a clearer sound.

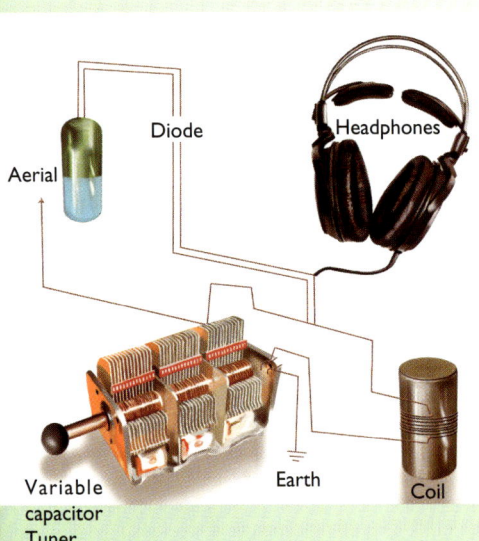

22

The Sound of Music

Any sound that is pleasant to the ear is musical. Musical sounds have wave patterns that are evenly spaced. This means that the number of vibrations made by a musical sound wave in one second is fixed. In other words, each musical note has a definite frequency of vibration. A sharp or a high pitch note has a higher frequency than a low pitch note.

Musical notes also have the same amplitude or loudness.

How musical are you?

1. Record a note of a particular frequency produced by different types of string (e.g. violin, guitar), percussion (tabla, drum) and wind (flute, trumpet) instruments.
2. Play them one after the other. Do they sound the same? What then distinguishes the various instruments?

No instrument can produce a pure note. Along with a note, all musical instruments produce a number of tones that are multiples of the frequency of the note. Different instruments produce different number of tones. This gives the variation in the quality of the sound.

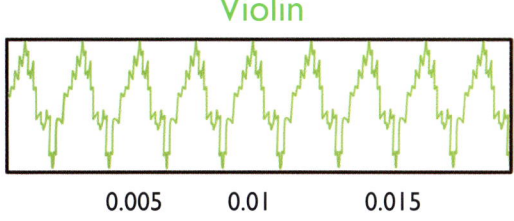

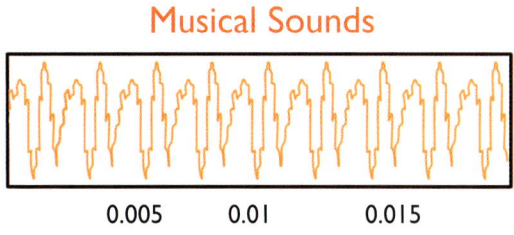

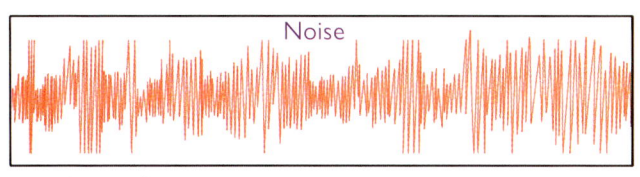

Sound box

Most musical instruments have something to amplify the sounds they make. Have you noticed the hollow wooden box of a guitar? The strings are attached to this sound box. When you pluck the strings, the vibrations make the wood and the air inside the box vibrate at the same frequency. This is called *resonance*. It makes the sound louder and richer.

Stretched strings

You will need:

- a wooden plank of dimensions 1" × 6" × 3"
- a long strong wire. (Try to get one from a shop that makes musical instruments.)
- a nail
- a hammer
- two small pieces of wood to use as props
- a small bucket
- some bricks or stones

Let us find out what happens to the sound made by a string when it is stretched.

1. Fix the nail on one end of the plank.
2. Place the plank on one corner of a table. Tie one end of the wire to the nail. Pull the other end over the plank.
3. Tie the bucket to this end of the wire. The bucket should hang freely. This will keep the wire stretched.
4. Insert the props so that the string does not touch the wooden plank and hence can vibrate freely.
5. Pluck the string in the middle and listen to the note.
6. Put a few stones in the bucket. This will stretch the wire further. Pluck the string again. Is there any change in the pitch of the sound?
7. Change the weights and note the changes in frequency.
8. What happens if you change the distance between the props?

To know more about stretched strings, let us make some simple musical instruments.

A rubber band guitar

You will need:

- a cardboard box
- 8 rubber bands of different thickness
- 2 wedge-shaped pieces of wood
- a pair of scissors

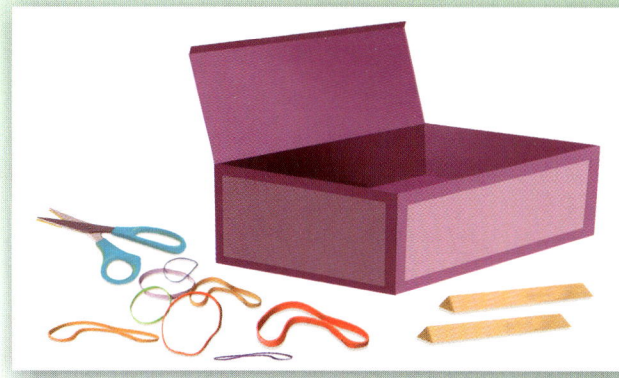

1. Cut out a hole in the lid of the box.
2. Stretch the rubber bands across the box as shown in the picture.
3. Insert the wedges under the bands.
4. Play your guitar.
   Do you notice any difference in the pitch of the sounds produced when you pluck the bands of different thickness?
5. Place a finger in the middle of a band, and pluck it. Has the pitch changed? Is it true that as the plucked string gets shorter, the pitch gets higher?

Try out this modification

1. Use rubber bands of the same thickness.
2. Place the wooden wedge in a slanted manner so that you have varying lengths of string.
3. Pluck the strings and listen to the notes produced.
4. Change the angle of the wedge. Does this change the pitch of the notes?
5. Tie knots to tighten the bands. This will give a sharper sound.

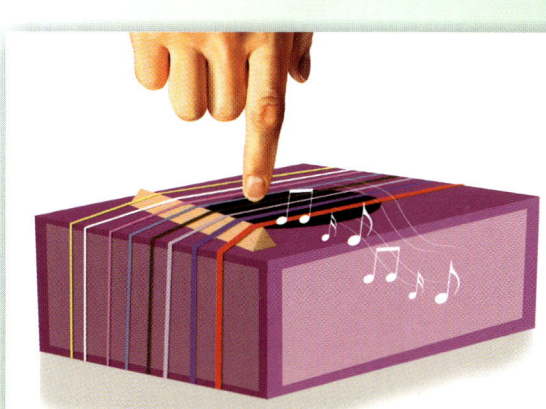

A twin-string banjo

You will need:

- a wooden piece of 1" × 1" × 3'
- a large empty plastic container with lid
- two wires of different thicknesses, each about 3' long
- two small blocks of wood
- four screw eyelets
- a knife
- sellotape
- a sea shell

1. Cut out two square holes on the opposite sides of the container just below the lid.
2. Push the long wooden piece through the holes as shown in the figure and tape it firmly in place.
3. Screw two eyelets at each end of the wooden board. Tie the wires between the eyelets as shown.
4. Place the wooden blocks so that the wires are not in touch with the board and can be strummed freely.
5. Tighten the strings by screwing up the eyelets.
6. Get a sea shell with a sharp edge. It will serve as your plectrum for strumming the banjo.
7. Hold down the strings with a finger at different places to get different notes.

Wind instruments

Instruments which musicians blow into, are called wind instruments. These instruments produce a note when the air inside them vibrates. The frequency of the vibrations depends on the length of the air column inside the instrument. The shorter the air column, the higher the pitch of the note produced.

A bottle organ

You will need:

- 8 bottles of the same shape and size
- water

1. Fill the bottles with different amounts of water.
2. Blow across each bottle in turn. You will notice that the higher the water level, the higher the notes.
3. Adjust the water levels in the bottles to get a musical scale.

Make your own pan pipe

You will need:

- six pieces of hollow bamboo pipes
- modelling clay
- sellotape
- a pair of scissors

1. Cut out the pipes into lengths ranging from 2-8 inches.
2. Seal one end of each pipe with modelling clay.
3. Arrange the pipes in order of length so that the open ends are exactly at the same level. Tape them firmly in position.
   Your pan pipe is ready.
4. To play, blow gently across the top of the pipe. Now try to figure which of the pipes produce higher notes – the longer or the shorter ones?

Make a glass xylophone

1. Take four tall glasses.
2. Fill one glass with water almost to the top. Make the second glass two-thirds full, the third glass one-third full, and keep the fourth glass empty.
3. To play the xylophone, tap the side of the glasses very gently with a wooden spoon. Each glass will produce a different note.
4. For better effect, use a set of china bowls and a pair of chopsticks.

Make a drum

You will need:

- an empty plastic bowl
- a plastic carry bag
- sellotape
- a pair of scissors
- thin sticks

1. Spread out the carry bag to form a large sheet.
2. Place the plastic bowl on the sheet and cut around it, keeping an extra margin of three inches.
3. With a friend's help, cover the mouth of the bowl with the plastic sheet and tape it in place. The plastic skin should be stretched as tightly as possible, without any wrinkles.
4. To play the drum, beat gently with the sticks.
5. Make drums with rubber sheets, leather or hard paper, and note the difference in sound.
6. How does the sound change with the size and the material of the bowl?

A Noisy World

We have already learnt that any unpleasant sound is called noise. To be a little more precise, a noise can be defined as sound made by an irregular pattern of waves.

The loudness of a noise is found by measuring the energy of a sound wave. It is usually measured in decibels. Our ears cannot detect a sound of zero decibels, while sounds above 140 decibels are dangerous to the unprotected ear. That is why people working with noisy machines are supposed to wear special ear pads to protect their ears from getting damaged.

How noisy is it?

How noisy do you think are the following things? Arrange them in ascending order of loudness to form a noise-scale chart.

1. a blaring loudspeaker
2. an exploding cracker
3. a motorbike without a silencer
4. laughter
5. a sawing machine
6. rustling leaves
7. an aeroplane
8. a rocket

Did you know?

Did you know that too much noise can permanently damage our hearing?
Think of ways to make our world less noisy and more peaceful.

Blank fire

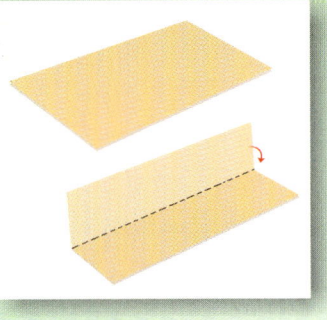 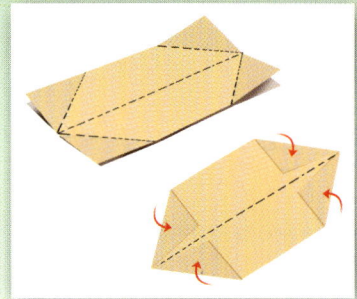 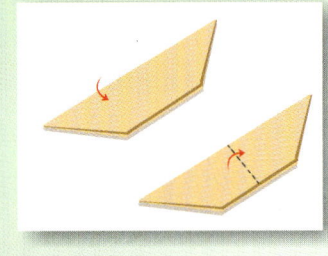  

You can make a paper pistol just by folding a piece of paper a few times over.

1. Take a rectangular piece of paper. Fold it in half along the longer side and open it out again.
2. Fold in the corners to meet the line of the centrefold.
3. Fold the paper in half as shown.
4. Fold in half, press firmly and open out.
5. Fold the ears down, as shown.
6. Fold back to make a triangular shape.
7. To fire your pistol, hold it between your fingers by the long ends, and flip it down fast.

A noisy boom

Supersonic aircrafts, like the concorde, fly at speeds faster than the speed of sound. When a concorde reaches the speed of sound and crosses it, a huge noise, the sonic boom, is produced. The noise has enough force to shatter windows!